ACTION

REPLACE FOSSIL FUELS

RESCUE DIGITAL DEVICES

GO TREE FREE

REUSE WOOD

HELP KEEP THE OCEAN HEALTHY

WHAT A WASTE

9 Ways to Fight Climate Change

KAREN TAM WU

illustrated by

BITHI SUTRADHAR

ORCA BOOK PUBLISHERS

To my past 10-year-old self. The term climate change was just becoming common when I was in elementary school. I would have loved a book like this. To all the kids today and tomorrow, may you feel compelled and inspired to act.

Published in Canada and the United States
in 2025 by Orca Book Publishers.
orcabook.com

Library and Archives Canada Cataloguing in Publication
Title: What a waste : 9 ways to fight climate change / Karen Wam Wu ; illustrated by Bithi Sutradhar.
Names: Tam Wu, Karen, author. | Sutradhar, Bithi, illustrator.
Description: Series statement: Orca take action ; 2 | Includes bibliographical references and index.
Identifiers: Canadiana (print) 20240498208 | Canadiana (ebook) 20240498216 | ISBN 9781459840447 (hardcover) | ISBN 9781459840454 (PDF) | ISBN 9781459840461 (EPUB)
Subjects: LCSH: Climate change mitigation—Juvenile literature. | LCSH: Conservation of natural resources—Juvenile literature. | LCSH: Waste minimization—Juvenile literature. | LCGFT: Instructional and educational works.
Classification: LCC TD171.75 .T36 2025 | DDC j363.738/746—dc23

Library of Congress Control Number: 2024949203

Summary: Part of the nonfiction Orca Take Action series for middle-grade readers, this illustrated book examines practical ways waste can be transformed to protect the planet and fight the effects of the climate crisis.

Orca Book Publishers is committed to reducing the consumption of nonrenewable resources in the production of our books. We make every effort to use materials that support a sustainable future.

Orca Book Publishers gratefully acknowledges the support for its publishing programs provided by the following agencies: the Government of Canada, the Canada Council for the Arts and the Province of British Columbia through the BC Arts Council and the Book Publishing Tax Credit.

Cover and interior artwork by Bithi Sutradhar.
Design by Troy Cunningham.
Edited by Kirstie Hudson.

Printed and bound in South Korea.

28 27 26 25 • 1 2 3 4

CONTENTS

INTRODUCTION

Environmental issues and taking care of the planet have been a passion of mine since I was a kid. I was active in my school's environmental club. I became a vegetarian when I was 12 after learning about the huge amount of water and land required to feed animals. I'm an avid recycler and rescuer of waste—whether it's food other people don't want or plastic bags and containers that could be reused. Repairing, reusing and repurposing the massive amounts of waste we make has always fascinated me. I think it's a way of fighting climate change that is often overlooked.

Many people of all ages feel helpless in the face of the climate crisis, but I'll introduce you to some inspiring waste-transforming innovations from around the world. You'll discover places where laws require reusing rather than wasting the planet's resources. And there are companies that have developed climate-friendly ways to make products from garbage. You'll meet scientists, innovators and leaders whom I met along the way. I hope this book leaves you feeling optimistic and gives you ideas on how to take action for the planet and be a waste warrior.

Protecting the Land

Do you know that parts of your computer come from nature? In fact, so does your toothbrush. I don't mean they grew out of the ground (but that would be amazing). Your computer is made from lots of metals and minerals found in the earth. The plastic in your toothbrush is made from fossil fuels. Fossil fuels also provide energy to heat homes and buildings, move people, and make and ship goods. These resources and all the stuff they're made into are also huge sources of waste.

Digging these resources out of the ground impacts the climate and environment. Roads are built and land is cleared to get fossil fuels, minerals and metals out of the ground. This can harm wildlife and fish habitat. Large amounts of water and energy are also used to extract fossil fuels, minerals and metals and turn them into useable forms. Mining and fossil fuel extraction often happen close to Indigenous communities, usually without consultation and partnership. Industrial activity can be harmful to these communities and their traditional lands. Some communities, particularly in the less wealthy countries, may not have laws to protect workers' health and safety.

Despite all the challenges, there are people working on solutions to decrease mining and create alternative sources of energy with the waste we make every day.

The burning of fossil fuels is the biggest cause of climate change.

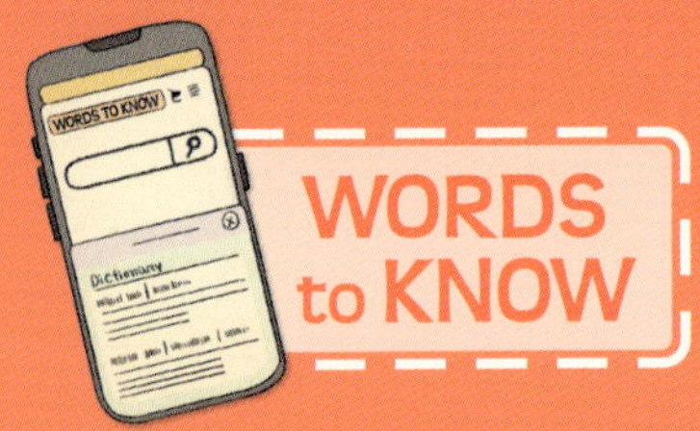

WORDS to KNOW

Carbon footprint:
the total amount of carbon pollution created from activities like driving or manufacturing

Carbon pollution:
carbon in the form of carbon dioxide (CO_2) or methane that is released into the air from the burning of fossil fuels for human activities like driving or manufacturing

Fossil Fuels:
fuels formed from the remains of plants and animals that have been buried for millions of years in Earth's crust. The most common types of fossil fuels are natural gas (also called fossil gas), oil (also called crude oil or petroleum) and coal.

Greenhouse Gas:
abbreviated as GHG, a gas that traps Earth's heat in the atmosphere, causing the planet's overall temperature to rise, rather than allowing the heat to radiate out to space. Carbon dioxide, methane and water vapor are the most abundant GHGs, but GHGs include nitrous oxide and fluorinated gases (used in refrigerators and air conditioners, for example). Human activity is responsible for the huge increase of carbon dioxide and methane in the atmosphere.

Canada is one of the largest producers of hydroelectricity (water power) in the world. You would think that means we would be less dependent on fossil fuels. But Canada and the United States consume the most fossil fuels per person per year, compared to all other countries in the world, which is nearly four times more than the global average. Yikes!

ACTION ONE: Replace Fossil Fuels

Our basic needs of eating and pooping generate waste. Americans create an astonishing amount of food waste every year, more than the UK, Germany, Italy, France and Sweden combined. More than half of the food wasted ends up in the landfill. Organic waste like food scraps rots in landfills and releases ***methane***. Methane is a greenhouse gas. The good news is that both food waste and human poop can be recovered and converted into ***biofuel***. Making biofuels is a way we can use fewer fossil fuels.

The average Canadian household generates 174 pounds (79 kilograms) of food waste per year, mostly fruits and vegetables. More than CAD $1,700 is spent on groceries that are never eaten. In the United States nearly 25 percent of all garbage that ends up in landfills is food. Food is the most common type of waste.

FUEL with FOOD SCRAPS

Have you ever wondered where the uneaten bits from your lunch or the leaves you helped rake go after you put them in your green garbage bin? In Surrey, British Columbia, that waste is turned into fuel. Organic waste like food scraps, leaves and grass clippings, from homes and businesses in Surrey and other nearby cities, is taken to the Surrey Biofuel Facility. It's sorted to be sure it doesn't contain any unwanted bits of plastic, metal and glass. The waste is then shredded and mixed with water to turn it into a slurry, or a kind of "soup." This soup is stored in an environment without oxygen to produce ***biogas***. Biogas must be purified before use. Then it is called ***biomethane***. The amount of biomethane made at the facility is enough to fuel all the trucks that collect organic waste from the entire region. The facility is still in its growing phase. In the future it will be able to make enough biomethane to run several thousand trucks a year!

After the biomethane is collected, ***compost*** is made from the soup. Rich in nutrients, compost is a superfood for gardens. The compost from the Surrey facility is used on local farms and for landscaping.

HEAT with POOP

When residents in Richmond, British Columbia, flush the toilet, they're helping heat their city with fewer fossil fuels. Wastewater and ***sewage*** from the city are collected at a treatment facility on Lulu Island. Treating wastewater creates biogas (like that at the Surrey Biofuel Facility).

An average adult produces over 300 pounds (136 kilograms) of poop per year. The value of human poop converted to fuel could be worth billions of dollars!

On Lulu Island, the biogas is captured under a large inflatable dome. The amount of biogas created here could warm and supply hot water to 600 homes. Treated sewage itself is warm. The facility uses the warmth from the sewage—considered waste heat—to heat the inside of the building. They're heating the plant with processed poop!

There's a lot of untapped energy in the warmth of poop. In the next few years, as more people move to the neighborhood around Oval Village in Richmond, the city plans to use waste heat from the sewer main to provide most of the energy needed for heating, cooling and hot water.

LIMITED EDITION

Unfortunately, we don't eat and poop enough to make the amount of biomethane we would need to replace the natural gas we currently use to heat our homes. Also, biomethane is a fuel that is combusted, or burned. Combustion creates carbon dioxide. Biomethane is like a "limited edition" fuel that should be saved for very specific uses, like in heavy trucks or for industrial uses.

Replacing fossil fuels with food scraps, poop and waste heat transformed into energy, like they do in Surrey and Richmond, is gentler on the land. It means fewer fossil fuels are used for heating. As an added bonus, keeping residential organic waste out of landfills means we are not creating methane. Using fewer fossil fuels means less need to dig up the land to extract them. It also means we are creating less carbon pollution.

South Korea has banned food waste going to landfills since 2005. Discarded food is turned into fertilizer, animal feed or biomethane used to heat homes.

- First, find out how much energy from fossil fuels or electricity you use in your home and to get to and from school, work and play. You can also use a carbon calculator (see Resources section).
- Put on a sweater. Heating is where we use the most energy in our homes. And heat that comes from ***fossil gas*** is a common form of energy used to heat homes. Turning down the temperature in your home is a way to use less energy. Talk to your parents or guardians about ways to make your home more ***energy efficient***. Maybe you could plan to switch to an electric heat pump. Reducing energy also means saving money.
- Drive less. If you can, walk, bike, take transit or carpool. You could talk about whether your family's next car or your school's next bus could be electric. Using less gas means—yup—saving money.
- Eat less meat, waste less food and compost your food waste. The production of dairy and meat creates a lot of greenhouse gases (GHGs). Fertilizers, land clearing (for grazing and growing crops) and cattle burps and farts are sources of GHGs, including methane.

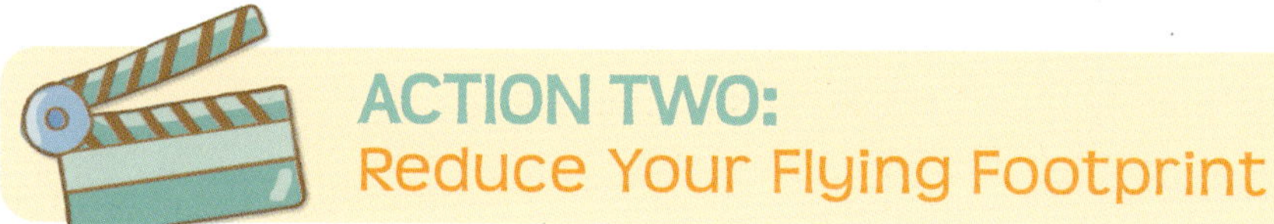

ACTION TWO: Reduce Your Flying Footprint

Flying produces about 2 percent of global greenhouse gas emissions. This doesn't sound like much, but emissions from planes are increasing at a faster rate than those from other forms of transportation. You might think the simple solution is to reduce the amount of flying everyone does, but for various personal and work-related reasons—like visiting family or traveling for business—people find it hard to give up flying. In fact, air travel is expected to double in the next 15 years.

In November 2023 a Virgin Atlantic Boeing 787 powered by 70 tons (63.5 metric tons) of a fuel made from waste vegetable oils, animal fats and fermented sugars flew from New York to London. This was the world's first commercial airliner to complete a transatlantic flight using 100 percent renewable diesel.

WHERE DOES CARBON POLLUTION COME FROM?

CANADA	UNITED STATES
31% Producing oil and gas	29% Cars and trucks
Cars and trucks 22%	25% Making electricity (using fossil fuels)
Heating homes and buildings 20%	23% Making chemicals, fossil fuels, metals and cement
Making metals, cement and paper 11%	13% Heating homes and buildings
Growing food (animals and crops) 10%	Growing food (animals and crops) 10%
Making electricity (using fossil fuels) 7%	

Planes that can fly long distances pollution-free are still many years away. Until then, it's important to reduce carbon pollution from planes and use fewer fuels extracted from the earth to make their engines run. My home province of British Columbia is one of the few places in the world where airplanes are required to use some renewable fuel every time they fill up. Starting in 2028, planes filling up in the province must contain at least 1 percent renewable fuel.

FLY with BURGERS and FRIES

The most common type of renewable jet fuel is made from pork, beef or chicken fat, and used cooking oil. It's called ***renewable diesel***. This fuel has a smaller carbon footprint than regular jet fuel. Renewable diesel can be substituted for regular jet fuel without modifying an airplane's engine.

Sources: (Canada) canada.ca/en/environment-climate-change/services/climate-change/greenhouse-gas-emissions/sources-sinks-executive-summary-2024.html#toc7; (US) epa.gov/ghgemissions/inventory-us-greenhouse-gas-emissions-and-sinks

A small amount of renewable diesel is made in my neighborhood. A local rendering plant picks up animal by-products—the parts of animals that aren't eaten—from farms and grocery stores. It also collects waste oil from restaurants. At the rendering plant, heads, guts, bones, blood and feathers are cooked down (rendered). The rendered oil and fat are then sent to a refinery close by to be made into renewable jet fuel.

In the United States, the company Neste has been making renewable fuels from waste cooking oil for many years. Trucks collect waste oil from thousands of restaurants, hotels, sports venues and food courts across the country. This waste oil is processed into renewable fuel, including fuel for airplanes.

USE WITH CAUTION

Renewable diesel made from waste oil can be far less harmful to the environment. But, as is the case with biomethane, it's difficult to make enough renewable jet fuel to replace all the regular jet fuel used today. For these reasons, flying will still be a major source of carbon pollution for many years to come. In the meantime, next time you're in a plane or see one in the sky, just remember that a little part of your bacon cheeseburger and fries may be powering that plane.

Find out if your community, province/state or country has a climate plan that reduces greenhouse gases and encourages a switch from fossil fuels to clean renewable energy. Ask your parent or guardian to help, or maybe you can suggest creating one as a class project.

If there is a climate plan:

- Does the plan commit to reduce carbon pollution by a specific amount (e.g., millions of tons or MT) by a certain deadline (e.g., 2030, 2050)?
- Has the government set aside money to pay for its plan?
- Are there ways to check that the government is sticking to its promise? For example, does the government or an independent group of experts publish a report card?
- Where could there be improvements, or what's missing? Write to your elected officials and let them know what you think.

If there's no plan, let your government know it's time to act.

ACTION THREE: Rescue Digital Devices

Next time you want to make fun of your parent's or guardian's phone because it's soooo old-school, think about this: North Americans are among the top generators of electronic waste (e-waste) in the world, and only around 20 percent of global e-waste is recycled! Electronics contain toxic chemicals such as lead and arsenic. When electronics are tossed in the garbage these chemicals can harm the health of humans and animals.

Our electronics contain valuable metals and minerals like silver, gold, platinum and copper. Lithium and ***rare-earth elements*** are among the ***critical minerals*** found in electronic devices. These minerals are used in clean energy technology, such as making batteries for electric vehicles. Valuable metals and critical minerals are worth recovering.

Many electronic devices and appliances that are thrown in the garbage or even recycled can actually be repaired. Extending the life of electronic devices is a way to reduce the need to mine the land for new materials.

REVIVE OLD COMPUTERS

Passing along a repaired computer will keep e-waste out of the landfill and help out someone who doesn't have the money for a brand-new computer. It's not uncommon for many of us to own more than one digital device. Watching a movie on your iPad, or looking up something on your

More than 68 million tons (62 million metric tons) of e-waste are generated globally every year. That's more than the weight of 8 million African elephants!

computer or a phone whenever you want, is maybe something you take for granted.

Yet millions of Americans and Canadians do not have access to high-speed internet at home and/or do not own a computer. The lowest-income households—Black, Indigenous (especially First Nations who live on reserves), people of color (BIPOC), individuals over 65, and people who live in rural areas—are most often the ones without access to these technologies.

These days access to a computer and the internet is essential. You need a computer to do your homework, keep in touch with family and friends, and apply for jobs.

Organizations like Electronics Recycling Association in Canada and Digitunity in the United States recover discarded computers and laptops. The devices are ***refurbished*** and donated to those in need. These organizations help reduce e-waste and get computers to those who need them.

REPAIR BEFORE REPLACING

Have you heard a grandparent or parent or guardian say, "They don't make things like they used to"? They're right. Manufacturers often purposefully make it hard to fix a device. This forces you to buy a new one even if all you really need is a new battery. The fix may require special tools, repair instructions may not be available, or the device may be digitally locked or physically difficult to open up.

There are organizations aiming to change that. The Restart Project in the United Kingdom, for example, runs workshops to teach people how to repair things. And the online community iFixit has developed thousands of free online manuals for repairing just about anything.

Alongside education, these organizations have been calling for right-to-repair laws. These laws would require manufacturers to make it easy for consumers to repair everything from cell phones to automobiles themselves or take them to a repair shop to be fixed.

But when devices are truly at the end of their lives, we need to make it easier to extract the valuable materials from them to reduce the need to mine more minerals. And to protect the environment, we need to dispose of nonrecyclable materials safely.

- Buy less stuff. It's that simple. Making new goods requires energy.
- Try repairing something that's broken before replacing it.
- Consider buying things secondhand.

LOVE-ESE CHILE

WHO: Love-Ese Chile is a research scientist and the former head of Regenerative Waste Labs.

WHAT: Studies new kinds of nature-based plastics to see how they break down in ***compost***. These are plastics made from things like seaweed, mushrooms and shells from shrimp and crabs.

WHERE: Lives and works in Vancouver, BC.

REMEMBERS THINKING: "When I grow up, I want to be an astronaut!"

HOBBIES: Gardening, mushroom hunting and whittling.

FUN FACT: Tiny organisms in compost can heat it up to 158°F (70°C). That's the same temperature as a mug of hot chocolate! They need these high temperatures to break down stuff like branches and other compostable products.

WASTE-WARRIOR TIP: Love-Ese saves bacon grease to make soap and uses citrus peels to create a natural cleaner. It's a neat way to transform kitchen scraps into something practical.

Protecting Forests

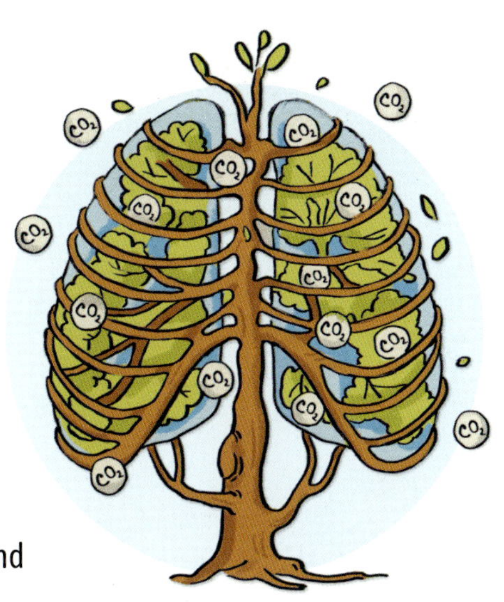

Forests are complex ecosystems that have evolved over centuries. They are the lungs of our planet, absorbing carbon dioxide and producing oxygen through ***photosynthesis***. Trees store carbon in their trunks, branches, leaves and roots. Stands of trees left to grow continue to absorb carbon over time. This makes forests important carbon sinks as well. This carbon is released slowly when a tree dies and decomposes.

WORDS to KNOW

Biodiversity:
(also biological diversity) the variety of all living things in nature. Greater biodiversity is a sign of health.

Carbon sinks:
locations in nature, such as forests, soil and the ocean, that absorb and store more carbon from the atmosphere than they release

Closed loop:
a system in which the material in a used product is reclaimed and made into something new. This cycle can occur over and over again.

Ecosystems:
communities of living, interacting organisms and their physical environment

Forests cover almost one-third of Earth's land. More than half of the world's forests are found in just five countries: Canada, the United States, Brazil, Russia and China.

When an ancient forest is logged to make products like toilet paper, pizza boxes or paper bags, all that carbon storage is gone. True, trees will grow back. But once old forests are logged, the huge amount of carbon the trees were storing will not be accumulated again in our lifetimes.

Forests also play an important role in moderating global temperatures and climate. There are very few places left on Earth where large forested areas have never been logged. These special forests are sometimes called ancient, old-growth or intact primary forests. These forests are our best hope for fighting climate change.

You can see why forests are so important for a healthy planet. Today there are companies that recognize this and take a different approach to using wood and fiber from forests. They've also come up with innovative tree-free alternatives for paper, buildings and clothing.

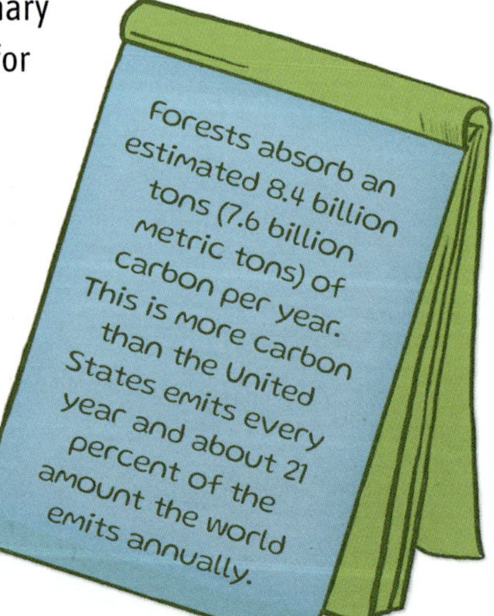

ACTION FOUR: Go Tree-Free

> Every year, 3.1 billion trees are logged to make paper packaging. Paper packaging makes up about one-third or more of household waste in Canada.

Oops, did you forget to bring your reusable bags to the grocery store? No problem—you were probably offered a paper bag instead of plastic. That seems like a good thing, right? Using less plastics made from fossil fuels is critical.

In the many countries where single-use plastic grocery bags are banned, including Canada and parts of the United States, paper bags have replaced the plastic ones. Plastic cartons and bottles are also starting to be replaced with paper-based packaging. But paper-based packaging is most commonly made from virgin fiber, which comes directly from trees rather than from fiber made with recycled paper or cardboard.

We are not solving the climate crisis if we continue to log our forests to make things like toilet paper and pizza boxes. Forests are the lungs and carbon banks of our planet.

REACH for RECYCLED

Paper and cardboard are among the most recycled materials in the world, and demand for recycled content is growing. Paper can be recycled six or seven times before the fibers become too short to stick together. After that, new virgin fiber needs to be added to the mix.

> Using recycled paper to make new paper products uses about half the amount of water and almost one-third less energy than making them with virgin fiber.

With improved paper-recycling techniques, we don't need to rely on virgin wood fiber to make magazines, books and notepads. You can find forest-friendly newspapers, toilet paper and cardboard boxes made with recycled paper. If you're using tissue with recycled content, you might be blowing your nose with a small part of your cereal box from last year! Paper of a higher quality, such as office paper, card stock and that used in some notebooks, is also being made with recycled fiber. This book is printed on paper with 30 percent recycled content.

Improving municipal recycling collection programs will increase the amount of clean recycled paper products available to paper producers. Setting a minimum amount of recycled content for paper products will lead to their containing more recycled material. Both of these actions will help keep paper products out of landfills and protect forests. But ultimately we need to cut down on our consumption of paper products, especially single-use items that get tossed after one use.

ASK for SHEETS of WHEAT

The next best option for forest-friendly paper is to make it using the straw left over after harvesting wheat, flax or other crops. Straw from crops grown to feed people or livestock can be made into fiber for paper. Imagine if the straw for the paper in this book and the wheat for your sandwich bread came from the same field!

Agricultural waste is often burned, which releases carbon dioxide into the atmosphere, or sent to a landfill, where it produces methane. Repurposing the leftover plant waste also means reducing greenhouse gas emissions, and that's good for the planet.

With all the benefits, why aren't we seeing more paper made with agricultural waste? One reason is that there are only a few facilities in the world where agricultural waste can be turned into pulp for paper products. Red Leaf Pulp is planning to build Canada's first wheat-straw pulp mill in Regina, Saskatchewan. Another reason is cost. To create some types of paper, wheat fiber needs to be blended. Blending wheat fiber, which is a short fiber, with other longer fibers like hemp or flax gives the final product strength. These alternative fibers might not be readily available and can be more expensive than fiber from softwood trees. Unfortunately, that means companies will keep logging trees for virgin fiber instead.

If more consumers, like you, are aware of alternatives to virgin wood fiber and ask for them, suppliers will hopefully respond. Over time this will make recycled and alternative fiber papers more available and reduce the cost. I hope that one day this book can be printed on paper that doesn't come from tree fiber.

1. Reduce the amount of single-use paper products you use.
2. Prioritize the kind of paper products you buy.

- **BEST CHOICE:** Paper products made with with post-consumer recycled content or post-industrial waste.
- **SECOND-BEST:** Paper products made from agricultural waste like straw from wheat or flax.
- If recycled or tree-free alternatives are not available, look for wood or paper products that carry the Ancient Forest Friendly logo or are labeled FSC 100% (which means the product is made of 100% virgin material from Forest Stewardship Council-certified forests).

3. Recycle the paper you do use so it stays out of the landfill.

ACTION FIVE: Reuse Wood

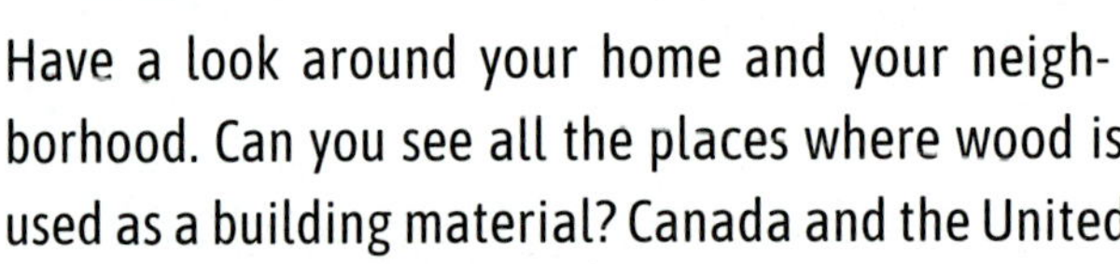

Have a look around your home and your neighborhood. Can you see all the places where wood is used as a building material? Canada and the United States are among the top producers and consumers of wood products in the world. More than half of the United States' lumber comes from Canada.

I love wood in buildings. It looks beautiful and gives institutional buildings like offices and schools a welcoming atmosphere. In fact, studies have shown that using wood indoors has a calming effect on people. There are some great companies that are using wood wisely to take advantage of its benefits and reduce the need to log our forests.

DECONSTRUCT, NOT DEMOLISH

The ReUse People in the United States encourages the deconstruction of homes. Deconstructing a home means taking it apart carefully instead of demolishing it into bits and pieces that are taken to the landfill. Materials like wood flooring, studs and beams can be reused and repurposed. ReUse People has stores where they sell wood products such as cabinets, doors, flooring and lumber, as well as things like windows, lights and faucets, all of it recovered from deconstruction projects.

Indigenous Peoples steward more than one-quarter of the world's lands, which includes intact forests and ecosystems that are some of the most biodiverse on the planet.

Construction and demolition materials make up more than one-third of waste in Canadian landfills. Cities in British Columbia, like Burnaby, Victoria and Port Moody, along with San Francisco and Portland in the United States, have requirements to minimize or avoid demolition. In these cities, wood must be set aside for another purpose instead of being sent to the landfill. Researchers at Cornell University are investigating ways to design and construct buildings so they can be taken apart easily for reuse.

Write to your local, provincial/state and federal government representative.

Science and traditional Indigenous knowledge show that we need to protect half of Earth's natural ecosystems to safeguard biodiversity. In Canada, the federal government has made the commitment to protect 30 percent of the country's land, inland water, coastal and marine areas by 2030 (30 by 30). This includes protecting intact ancient forests. These ecosystems contain most of nature's water-storage system. Achieving 30 by 30 is key to the eventual goal of protecting half of the planet's ecosystems. Tell your member of Parliament and provincial representative that you'll be watching the government's progress in keeping this promise. In the United States, ask your representatives to follow Canada's example.

ACTION SIX: Reduce Clothing Waste

Check the labels on your clothes to see what they're made of. Did you find any made with polyester? Polyester, a plastic fiber made from oil, is the mostly widely used fiber in clothing today. The majority of clothes are made from a blend of materials that includes polyester. It's hard to reuse fiber from clothing made from a mix of materials. And polyester creates microplastics when it's washed, which take hundreds of years to decompose.

Clothes made from trees may seem like a more "sustainable" choice, because trees grow back, right? Chemically treated wood pulp can be spun into fiber for materials like viscose (also known as rayon). Viscose is used to make baby wipes, face masks, T-shirts, dresses and the linings of suits. The fiber to make viscose comes from tropical ***rainforests*** in Brazil and Indonesia and from ***boreal forests*** in Canada.

Tropical rainforests contain a huge amount of the planet's carbon and biodiversity. The planet's boreal forests, mostly found in Canada, are considered carbon "sponges," because of the vast amount of carbon they store. But climate change is fueling massive forest fires, which in turn, as they burn and release carbon dioxide into the air, feed climate change.

Tropical rainforests account for about 30 percent of the tree cover on the planet, but they contain 50 percent of the world's stored carbon and biodiversity. Different amounts of carbon are stored in parts of trees (like trunks and roots) and in forest soil depending on the type of forest and where in the world it grows.

Wood fiber and pulp are used in a lot of products you might not expect, like LCD screens (on cell phones and computers), toothpaste and flavoring in Doritos chips.

Logging these forests—which destroys precious habitat and releases carbon—for the sake of fashion doesn't make sense. Making viscose also uses a lot of energy and creates a lot of wastewater and solid waste. But one company has found a way to repurpose old clothes to make forest-friendly viscose.

WEAVE NEW CLOTHES from OLD

An old pulp mill in Sweden has been turned into a factory. Circulose gives old clothes new life. Used jeans and cotton T-shirts are shredded and then broken down through chemical processing into a watery mixture known as dissolving pulp. This is bleached, dried and pressed into thick paperlike sheets of pure cellulose, the fibrous part of plants that makes them stiff and strong. These sheets can be made into viscose fabric for making new clothes. In addition to reclaiming tossed clothing, this process also creates less waste, releases 5.5 tons (5 metric tons) less carbon per ton of material produced and uses 90 percent less water and fewer chemicals compared to viscose made from virgin fiber.

Did you know that it takes a lot of water to grow cotton and other fibers? Processing and dyeing fibers, both natural and synthetic, also use water (and create pollution as well). Clothing production is one of the "thirstiest" industries.

It is not sustainable to keep pumping oil to make polyester and cutting down trees to make viscose. We need to keep microplastics out of the ocean and clothes out of landfills. Fashion manufacturing must be a closed loop, where fabric from used clothing is reclaimed and used over and over again to create new fashions instead of being thrown away.

Of the estimated 100 billion items of clothing produced globally each year, 65 percent end up in the landfill within 12 months. Just 1 percent of recycled clothing is turned into new clothing.

- Reduce the amount of new clothing you buy.
- Buy secondhand clothes.
- Organize a clothing swap with your friends.

VALÉRIE COURTOIS

WHO: Valérie Courtois is the executive director of a nonprofit organization called the Indigenous Leadership Initiative. She is Innu, from the community of Mashteuiatsh.

WHAT: Valérie and her team work with First Nations communities to protect and look after lands and waters across Canada.

WHERE: Lives in Happy Valley-Goose Bay, on the eastern edge of the boreal forest in Newfoundland and Labrador.

REMEMBERS THINKING: "When I grow up...I'm going to work to protect the land. I absolutely knew this since I was 11."

HOBBIES: Cooking, crocheting, playing music and taking photos.

FUN FACT: Canada's boreal forest, which stretches from the Yukon to Labrador, is called a "forest of blue" because it holds 25 percent of the world's wetlands and more surface fresh water than anywhere else on Earth. Valérie says she loves the fact that it is home to so many food sources she enjoys, including caribou, beaver and porcupine.

WASTE-WARRIOR TIP: Valérie uses an ice auger her grandfather bought in the 1970s, which has been repaired many times over the years. Living in a remote region in the North means Valérie and her community have to be creative with materials and extend the life of them. It's practical, but it also allows for a more meaningful relationship with those materials.

Protecting Water

What do your toothbrush, milk jug and backpack have in common? If you guessed that they're all made from plastic, you're right. Plastic is everywhere. Plastic can be lightweight, strong, flexible and durable. It's also cheap to make. But plastic is hard on the planet, in particular the water on our planet. First, plastics are made from fossil fuels, and fossil fuels cause climate change. In turn, the warming planet is changing the hydrological cycle (a fancy term for water cycle) on Earth. Second, plastics are finding their way into our waterways, and many of them are ending up in the ocean. Today plastic is the most common type of waste found in oceans.

WORDS to KNOW

Footprint: the total amount of resources needed, whether energy or water, to provide a service or make a product. Having a large footprint means using a lot of resources and possibly having a negative effect on the environment.

Fresh water: water found in nature that is not salty, such as water from lakes, ponds, rivers and creeks

Wastewater: water that has been used for human activities at home or in the workplace, including such things as bathing, toilet flushing, washing clothes and dishwashing

All the water on our planet is connected. Fresh water flows to our oceans from rivers, streams, lakes and wetlands. Moisture from the ocean evaporates and falls as rain to replenish our freshwater sources. Oceans are like sponges that absorb and moderate heat and carbon dioxide levels. This "sponge" function has been critical to keeping Earth's temperature stable. Today, however, the oceans are having a hard time keeping up with the amount of carbon pollution and heat in our atmosphere.

We use water for drinking, cooking, bathing, growing food, producing energy, making and washing clothes and many other things. As the population of the planet increases, we'll use even more water in the years to come.

Oceans cover about 71 percent of Earth's surface. Of all the water on Earth, 97 percent is found in the oceans.

Climate change is decreasing Earth's supply of fresh water. Already there are areas of water scarcity. We must use water wisely to have enough to meet our needs today and in the future.

Already there are countries and cities around the world where people are reclaiming and reusing water. There are also people working on alternatives to plastic, some that come from the ocean itself.

Only about 3 percent of Earth's water is fresh. Canada, the United States, Brazil, Russia, Indonesia, China and Colombia have most of the world's surface fresh water.

ACTION SEVEN: Reduce Your Water Footprint

Have you noticed that seasonal weather patterns are changing? Maybe you get to wear T-shirts and shorts for more months of the year, or maybe you need to shovel snow more or less frequently in the winter. As the planet warms, Earth's water cycle is changing and becoming less predictable. Snow in the mountains is melting earlier. This causes creeks and rivers to reach their highest levels earlier in the spring. Some parts of the world are seeing higher amounts of rain than usual, which are sometimes causing floods. In other places, the dry season is lasting longer and there's much less precipitation, making the soil extremely dry and creating drought. All of this means we need to change how we use water.

Can you guess what humans use the most water for? About 70 percent of Earth's fresh water is used to grow food. Rice, soybeans and wheat, in particular, require a lot of water. The growing of crops like corn, hay and alfalfa, to feed and provide water to cows, chickens and other livestock, is also water-intensive.

In the Pacific Northwest, we've had drought conditions for the past few summers (even though we are surrounded by rainforest)! That made me want to be more thoughtful about my water use. In the dry summer months, I collect the water I use for rinsing dishes or washing hands in a portable basin in the kitchen sink. I then dump this water on the fruit trees and veggies in our garden. After I started doing this, I learned that entire countries are collecting and reusing wastewater in much the same way.

RECLAIM WATER for AGRICULTURE

In places where less water is available, people are forced to find solutions to the water shortage. In Israel, the dry climate is not naturally suitable for agriculture, but through reclaiming wastewater, the country has overcome this challenge. Today Israel is a world leader in water reuse, reclaiming nearly 90 percent of its wastewater for agricultural use. First the water from washing dishes and clothes, bathing, and flushing the toilet is collected. This water goes through an extensive treatment system, starting with the removal of solid human waste and food scraps. Then tiny organisms like friendly bacteria and

> The United Arab Emirates is the highest consumer of water per person per day. The United States and Canada take second and third place, respectively.

protozoa (tiny single-celled animals) break down sugars, fats, human waste, food, soaps, detergents and other molecules. Lastly the water is filtered and purified. The purified water is piped to farms throughout the country. Israel has become a major exporter of fresh produce by using reclaimed wastewater and special farming techniques.

In comparison, less than 10 percent of city wastewater in the United States is reused. What we in North America consider "wasted" water, Israelis consider a valuable resource to reclaim.

- **REDUCE YOUR WATER FOOTPRINT BY CHOOSING CAREFULLY WHAT YOU EAT.** Your food choices have the biggest impact by far on your water footprint. Farmed fish and prawns, cheese, milk, beef and pork require a lot of water to make. Choose foods that need less water to produce, such as oat or nut milk, tofu, beans and legumes.
- **DON'T WASTE FOOD.** Around a third of the food produced globally is never eaten. It's either spoiled while being transported or is thrown away by households, restaurants and grocery stores. That means the water it took to produce this food is also wasted. Wasting food also means wasting money.
- **USE LESS WATER.** Washing your clothes less often, taking shorter showers and using the dishwasher (instead of washing dishes by hand) are all ways to reduce water use at home. These actions also reduce the energy (often natural gas) used to heat the water. This isn't an excuse to skip showering or get out of the dishes, though.

ACTION EIGHT: Help Protect Fresh Water

All the water you use to flush the toilet, bathe and wash dishes and clothes goes down the drain and is not reused. For most of us in North America, the water that comes out of our taps, regardless of how we use it, is potable—which means it's clean enough to drink. We are very fortunate that most of us can access potable water with a turn of a tap. This is not something we should take for granted.

Every time you flush the toilet, up to 7 gallons (more than 26 liters) of drinkable water goes down the drain. That's like flushing away seven big milk jugs' worth of water!

My friend Tobita-san, who lives in Japan, has a sink that is integrated into the toilet. On a recent visit, as I washed my hands the water drained from the sink and filled the toilet tank, ready for the next flush. Some places have taken this super water-smart tap-to-toilet design to a whole new level.

In June 2024, Calgary residents had to reduce water consumption by at least 25 percent after the main pipe carrying water to the city broke. People used dishwater to flush toilets and collected water from showering to water gardens. They also collected rainwater from downspouts in whatever containers they had. One household even collected rainwater in a canoe.

PEE in the GARDEN

The city of San Francisco has taken the tap-to-toilet idea to the neighborhood scale. The city's philosophy is that water is too precious to use just once. For many years the city has required that large new buildings,

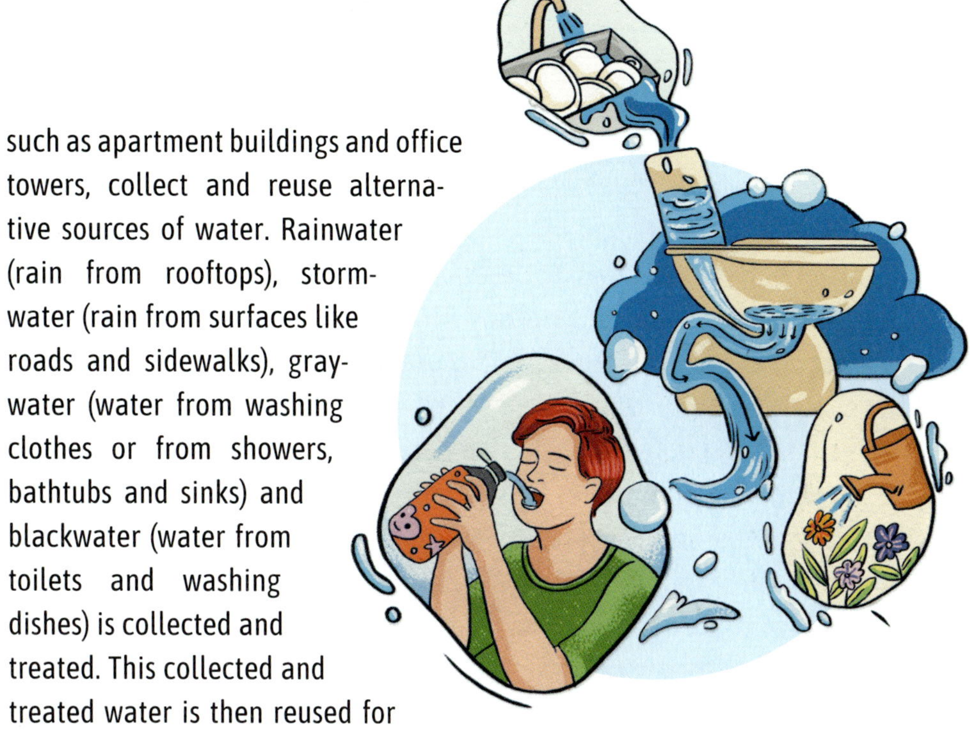

such as apartment buildings and office towers, collect and reuse alternative sources of water. Rainwater (rain from rooftops), stormwater (rain from surfaces like roads and sidewalks), graywater (water from washing clothes or from showers, bathtubs and sinks) and blackwater (water from toilets and washing dishes) is collected and treated. This collected and treated water is then reused for nonpotable uses like washing clothes, flushing toilets and watering plants outdoors. Reusing water reduces dependency on drinking water.

San Francisco is also using this tap-to-toilet design in a new neighborhood, Mission Rock. Once people and businesses have settled into Mission Rock, all of its non-potable water needs, such as watering gardens and parks and toilet flushing, will come from water that is reclaimed and treated on-site. In this neighborhood, the water you used to flush your toilet could be watering the park across the street.

Many Indigenous communities in Canada face challenges accessing safe drinking water as a result of colonization and discriminatory practices. In some communities, this has been the case for years or even decades.

SAVE WATER, DRINK PEE

Cities in Texas, Singapore, Belgium, the United Kingdom, Kuwait, Namibia, South Africa and Australia send water from the tap to the toilet and then back to the tap. This is an option in places where fresh water is very limited. Graywater and blackwater are reclaimed, treated, purified and returned to the drinking-water supply. Just think—in these places, the water you used to flush the toilet a month ago could be the water your mom makes coffee with tomorrow morning! In fact, you can tell the adults in your life that they can buy beer made with pee. For real! Several beers sold in the United States and Europe are proudly advertised to be made with recycled shower water and wastewater.

While "tap to toilet to tap" may sound gross, the water goes through a lot of treatment before becoming drinkable again. These cities are showing that recycled water can be safe and clean and help ease water shortages.

So far, most of North America hasn't been forced to recycle water this way. But we don't need to wait for severe conditions to change our relationship with water. We can start now.

Astronauts on the International Space Station reclaim and reuse 98 percent of the water used for food preparation, bathing and teeth brushing, along with water from their pee and sweat!

Be a water protector. Find out what kind of water-protection laws and policies your local/provincial/state/federal governments have in place. Are there laws that:

- protect the right to clean drinking water?
- ensure there's enough water in rivers and streams for fish to survive?
- ensure there's enough water in rivers and streams for growing food?
- protect entire watersheds and ecosystems when water is shared between many users?
- take into consideration the impacts of floods and drought, which become more extreme with climate change, on the needs of animals, ecosystems and humans?

ACTION NINE: Help Keep the Ocean Healthy

Plastic is one of the most common items we throw away. In the United States, an estimated 40 million tons (36 million metric tons) of plastic waste is generated each year. In Canada, plastic makes up one-third of the waste we throw away each year.

Many cities and towns across Canada collect plastic from homes as part of recycling programs. Much of this waste was sent overseas, often to China. But in 2018 China stopped accepting plastic waste. That means there aren't as many places to send our plastic waste as there used to be. In fact, many places around the world have inadequate programs to deal with plastic waste. Plastic, as we've already discovered, ends up in rivers and oceans, where it breaks down into very small pieces called microplastics.

These teeny bits of plastic can hinder drifting plants, algae and bacteria (collectively called plankton) from photosynthesizing and creating oxygen for our planet.

I'd always thought forests were the lungs of the planet, breathing in carbon dioxide and breathing out most of Earth's oxygen. Turns out, as much as 80 percent of Earth's oxygen comes from ocean plankton! But today our oceans—our other set of lungs—are choking on our plastic waste. Remarkably, the solution to our plastic problem may come from the ocean itself.

TURN SEAWEED into PLASTIC

Researchers and companies from all over the world, including in Canada, Europe, Asia and the United States, have been looking to the oceans for plastic substitutes. The alternatives could also help heal our oceans.

Soft and film plastic are among the most common types of plastic. They are used to wrap fruits and vegetables and package goods such as toothbrushes and toys. New companies in the United States and Europe, such as Sway and Notpla, are successfully using seaweed to make a new kind of bioplastic (plastic made from animal or plant material) to replace soft plastics made from oil.

Using seaweed has many benefits. Seaweed grows quickly and absorbs carbon dioxide, and farming it provides jobs to local communities. Researchers have been able to make bioplastics from an invasive type of seaweed called *Sargassum*. This seaweed has been piling up on beaches in the Caribbean and Gulf of Mexico. Removing some of it to create bioplastic will help restore marine ecosystems in those areas.

A bonus of seaweed-based plastic is that it can be dissolved in water or composted in your garden at home.

SUB OUT STYROFOAM

Chitin is a natural material found in the hard shells of sea creatures like crabs, lobsters and shrimps (and also, incidentally, in land-based critters like beetles and mealworms). Scientists and companies around the world are developing alternatives to Styrofoam. Styrofoam, which is made from fossil fuels, is extremely difficult to recycle. One option is to use waste shrimp shells and the shells of invasive crabs to make a compostable replacement for Styrofoam. Like seaweed-based plastics, chitin-based products can be dissolved or composted.

While we wait for alternatives to be more available, there are ways to cut down on the mountains of plastic waste we are creating. Clearly, we need to use less plastic. Having fewer types of plastic, all made with similar chemicals, would make it easier to sort and recycle plastics. And we also need to change our laws—banning single-use plastics everywhere, for example, and requiring manufacturers to use plastics that can be composted.

Reject, reduce or reuse plastic. This can be challenging, as plastic is everywhere, but start with simple things.

- Say "no thanks" when asked if you need a plastic bag (even for produce), straw or cutlery. Be the friendly "bag nag" and remind your family and friends to bring their own alternatives.
- Find ways to reduce or phase out plastic. For example, encourage your parents or guardians to buy bulk or loose unpacked goods (such as fruits and vegetables), shop at refill stores, and learn to make your own soap and yogurt.
- When you can't avoid taking or buying an item that comes in plastic, find ways to reuse it. At the end of its life, be sure to dispose of it responsibly. Hopefully there is recycling available.

DAVID KIM

WHO: David Kim is the the vice president of manufacturing at Hydrapak.

WHAT: David was part of the team that created one of the first reusable water bottles in North America made with 50 percent upcycled plastic. He decides how and where Hydrapak makes their products and delivers them to customers.

WHERE: Lives in Oakland, California, but divides his time between Hong Kong, Colorado and Oakland.

REMEMBERS THINKING: "When I grow up, I want to be a journalist. I loved reading newspapers when I was a kid."

HOBBIES: Building and riding all kinds of bikes—mountain, road and folding.

FUN FACT: Automated sorting machines in recycling plants can pick out small items like bottle caps (which go to the garbage).

WASTE-WARRIOR TIP: To help maximize the usefulness of items and reduce packaging waste, David suggests buying used instead of new. He buys secondhand cameras, lenses and, of course, bike frames and bike parts.

NOW WHAT?

I hope you can now look at waste with different eyes and see it as a valuable resource. Reusing, repurposing and repairing waste are important ways to fight climate change. Some simple actions to remember:

Buy less stuff.

Waste less water, energy and food. This saves money too!

Reuse more.

Be a waste warrior!

Glossary

BIOFUEL—fuel made from living matter, such as plants, algae or animal waste, not from fossilized plants and animals. It can be a solid, a liquid or a gas.

BIOGAS—a gas made from the breakdown of organic material such as food, plant material and manure

BIOMETHANE—methane that is left after carbon dioxide, hydrogen sulfide and water are removed from biogas

BOREAL FORESTS—forests of coniferous trees such as pines and spruce that grow in the northern half of the planet, where there are cold temperatures (Canada, Alaska and Russia)

COMPOST—broken-down organic material that is rich in nutrients and is often used in gardens

CRITICAL MINERALS—the minerals and metals needed to make clean energy technology, such as the lithium, nickel and zinc used to make electric car batteries and solar panels

ENERGY EFFICIENT—using less energy

FOSSIL GAS—another term for natural gas, to distinguish it from biogas and regular gasoline

METHANE—a gas made of one carbon atom and four hydrogen atoms (CH_4). It is the main component of natural gas and biomethane. Methane hangs out in the atmosphere for only 12 years compared to CO_2, which sticks around for hundreds of years. But during its short lifespan, methane traps more than 80 times as much heat as CO_2 does over a period of 20 years.

PHOTOSYNTHESIS—the process by which plants convert sunlight, carbon dioxide and water into energy and oxygen

RAINFORESTS—tall, dense forests that receive a lot of rainfall in a year. Lots of different species of plants and animals live in rainforests. Tropical rainforests are found in warm climates in the southern half of the planet. Temperate rainforests are generally found in coastal areas in the northern half of the planet.

RARE-EARTH ELEMENTS—a group of 17 elements that are components of such things as cell phones, computer hard drives and electric and hybrid vehicles. Also called rare-earth metals.

REFURBISHED—repaired and restored to proper working condition

RENEWABLE DIESEL—a biofuel made from vegetable oils and animal fats. It's chemically identical to fossil diesel and can replace fossil diesel in engines without modifying the engines. Biodiesel is also made from vegetable oils and animal fats but through a different process. This results in a fuel that is chemically different from fossil diesel. To be used in existing engines, biodiesel must be blended with fossil diesel in small amounts.

SEWAGE—human waste, as in pee and poop, that is carried away by sewers

Resources

Links to external resources are for personal and/or educational use only and are provided in good faith without any express or implied warranty. There is no guarantee given as to the accuracy or currency of any individual item. The author and publisher provide links as a service to readers. This does not imply any endorsement by the author or publisher of any of the content accessed through these links.

RECYCLING AND RESPONSIBLE DISPOSAL: Your city or other local government should have information on how to recycle goods and where/how to dispose of nonrecyclable waste for your local area.

CALCULATE YOUR CARBON FOOTPRINT: carbon-calculator.climatehero.org

CALCULATE YOUR WATER FOOTPRINT: watercalculator.org

FIND FOREST-FRIENDLY PAPER AND PAPER PRODUCTS: epd.canopyplanet.org

WHERE TO LEARN MORE FACTS: Ourworldindata.org has all sorts of graphs and charts that compare regions in terms of things like climate change impacts, energy use and access to clean water.

ORGANIZATIONS TO CHECK OUT: There are so many organizations doing amazing work locally, nationally and internationally. I list a few below to get you started and strongly encourage you to look up organizations in your neighborhood, city and province/state.

Canopy Planet
Canadian Parks and Wilderness Society
Digitunity
Electronic Recycling Association
Food Rescue Hero
iFixit
Keepers of the Water
The ReUse People
Second Harvest
Sierra Club
Waterkeeper Alliance

Acknowledgments

Thank you! I would never have imagined tackling such a project without the encouragement of Kirstie Hudson and the support of the whole team at Orca Book Publishers. I am in absolute awe at how Bithi Sutradhar made my words come to life through her beautiful illustrations. Suggestions from my childhood friend Wendy, and the work of my long-time friends Nicole Rycroft and Valerie Langer (at Canopy) to fight climate change as waste warriors, sparked the idea for this book. Valerie was a huge source of information for my research. Her fight to protect Clayoquot Sound was my inspiration to include Action Figures in the book. My dear friend Sarah was a great sounding board for ideas throughout the process. I'm grateful to all my young friends and their parents who shared their insights with me: Luca Z., Nina, André, Katie, Kian, Finlay, Conor, Bec, Luca R., Dominic, Nadia, Chloe, Ha, Scarlett and Mathew. Thank you to the various colleagues who were invaluable sources of technical clarification. Finally, I would not have been able to create this book without my partner's steadfast support throughout all our life's adventures and for (most of) my wild ideas. Ben, this book proves that coffee and croissants fuel creativity!

proheadshots.ca

Ever since she was a kid **KAREN TAM WU** has been an environmental advocate. At the age of 12, after learning about the huge amounts of water and land needed to raise livestock, Karen became vegetarian—and still is. Armed with a degree in forest conservation, Karen has spent many years working to promote and protect healthy ecosystems and the communities that depend on these ecosystems. Nowadays, Karen helps decision makers understand what kinds of programs, laws and technologies leaders around the world are using to reduce carbon pollution and create clean renewable energy. Karen lives in Vancouver, where she can smell cedars and the ocean, play in the mountains and ride her bike year-round.

BITHI SUTRADHAR is a Bangladeshi illustrator and graphic designer who holds a master of publishing degree from Simon Fraser University, as well as an MFA and BFA in graphic design from the University of Dhaka. Alongside her professional illustration work, Bithi enjoys sharing her knowledge and skills through teaching. Her contributions have been recognized by educational institutions and government bodies such as the Ministry of Agriculture in Bangladesh. In 2024, Bithi created the illustrations for the first three books in the Take Action series as part of an internship with Orca Book Publishers. Bithi lives in Vancouver and loves exploring the vibrant outdoor scenes in her spare time, finding inspiration in the city's natural beauty.

Anik Saha

TAKE
REDUCE YOUR
FLYING FOOTPRINT
REDUCE
CLOTHING
WASTE
HELP PROTECT
FRESH
FRESH
FRESH
FRESH
WATER
REUSE
WOOD
REDUCE
YOUR WATER
FOOTPRINT